Spithead!

by Charlotte McKee

illustrated by Linda Shaw

Elm Grove Publications
Waco, Texas

All Rights Reserved
Printed in the United States of America
copyright c 2024 by Charlotte McKee

No part of this publication
may be reproduced by any method
or for any use without prior written
permission from the publisher.

ISBN # 979-8-218-46848-4

Elm Grove Publications
Waco, Texas
https://www.elmgrovepub.com

This book is dedicated to my daughter
Jean Nicole Swann
and to my granddaughter
Eala Ann Vargas
who gave me the inspiration
to write this book.

This Isaac Newton quote is one of my favorite.

"To me I am only a child playing on the beach while vast oceans of truth lie undiscovered before me."

Spithead!

Historical Background

Woolsthorpe Manor near Lincolnshire, England was Isaac Newton's ancestral home, a farmstead raising sheep. He rebelled against a life spent "herding sheep and shoveling dung" and was sent to Trinity College, Cambridge University when he was seventeen years of age. He returned home as top of his class at age twenty-three when Cambridge closed its doors due to the Great Plague in London.

"Hey, Spithead!" Isaac calls when it's supper time.
"It's chilly out. Come on in." He opens his manor house door. "There's a fire in every room," he says.

Isaac pokes the fire and stirs it up. "School's out," he says. "The plague's in London! All the students have been sent home. Only us here, Spithead," he says. "Keep the doors closed. Don't let the cold air in."

Isaac slips away.
I hear the kitchen door close. Climbing the attic stairs, his footsteps fade away. Then, silence.

Here I am trapped in Isaac's hot, smoky kitchen. I wait. I tidy my whiskers and nap.

Three catnaps later Isaac opens the kitchen door.

He peeks downs at me. "Sorry, Spithead," he says. "Didn't mean to be gone so long."

ISAAC NEWTON FACTS

1. Isaac was born on Christmas Day 1642 in the town of Lincolnshire, England. This was the same year the great astronomer Galileo died.
2. He was born prematurely and after the death of his father.
3. Because he was so small he wasn't expected to live. In fact, his tiny body would fit into a quart mug.

I run and bump headfirst into Isaac's door. I meow that his door makes me a prisoner. How can we be friends? I try to explain.

But no. It's no use. He doesn't understand.
   "Look here, Spithead," Isaac says. "I understand plenty!"

You're an object in motion and will stay an object in motion until stopped by my door.
I'll call this my 1st Law of Motion."

I'm not impressed. Cats know all about motion.

Once more Isaac climbs the attic stairs. He does not forget me. Not this time. He brings me along.

Isaac pulls a curtain across the window. Darkness comes. He puts out the fire. The room cools. "I'm studying light," he says. "Keep the door closed. Don't let the daylight in."

Isaac gets busy. I cannot help myself. My nose opens the curtain just a little…

Suddenly, a beam of sunlight slams across the room. Then, it shoots its colors on the wall.

Isaac lets out a whoop! He jumps up and down.

People! This is my man, but he's not brilliant.

"Look there, Spithead," Issac points. "I'm brilliant. **White light, when it passes through a glass prism, divides itself into all the colors of the rainbow. I'll call this my Theory of Light.**"

I'm not impressed.

Cats know all about light.

ISAAC NEWTON FACTS

4. Isaac was reared by his grandmothers in a lonely farmstead named Woolsthorpe Manor House.
5. Isaac attended Trinity College in Cambridge.
6. Cambridge closed during the Great Plague of London. All students were sent home for eighteen months.

"Outside?" Isaac asks later.

He leaves me there. He forgets all about me. My heart breaks. I climb up high in the apple tree.

Isaac remembers me later and runs to find me. "Come down, Spithead! Forgive me," he begs. "I do want to be friends."

    I meow for Isaac to open his closed door. How can we be friends? If not, I'd just as soon live in a tree. I guess he's not as smart as a cat.

    "See here, Spithead," Isaac says. "I'm just as smart."

Isaac needs a lesson, so I bump an apple. It bounces off his head.

"I get it," Isaac says. He picks up the apple. His eyes squint and his head nods. He says, **"A force acted upon this apple. It fell from the tree. It's the same force that holds the moon in its orbit. I'll call it my Law of Gravity."**

I'm not impressed.

Cats know all about gravity.

But I am impressed with what Isaac does next. He saws a cat-sized hole in the bottom of his door. Right there! Then he attaches a leather flap so I can go back and forth. He invents a cat-flap door just for me.

Isaac can keep his doors closed, and we can be friends. I might be the first cat ever with a cat-flap door.

SPITHEAD FACTS:
1. Isaac and Spithead revised all the laws of science.
2. Isaac invented the cat-flap door for Spithead. He made a cat-sized hole in the bottom of his door. Then he attached a piece of leather so Spithead could go back and forth.
3. Spithead gave birth. Isaac made kitten-sized holes with kitten-flap doors right beside Spithead's. The kittens had their very own kitten-flap doors.

When the kittens come, Isaac runs to make a kitten-sized hole in each door beside Spithead's. Now, the kittens have their own kitten-flap doors.

Isaac must be the smartest man alive. Maybe that has ever lived. But all cats know he only needs to make one cat-flap door. Each kitten will follow mother cat through the same door.

Whatever. My Cat-Sense tells me Isaac is great. When he makes friends, he stops what he's doing to be with them.

I'll call this my 1st Law of Friendship.

the end

Isaac Newton found a hungry black cat on his doorstep. He brought it inside and named it Spithead. At that time cats were considered vermin: little better than the mice and rats they ate. Certainly, no one adopted them. The next eighteen months with Spithead were the most creative in Newton's life. He and his cat changed the world and revised all the laws of science.

Then he invented something for his beloved Spithead that has endured for centuries - a pet door.

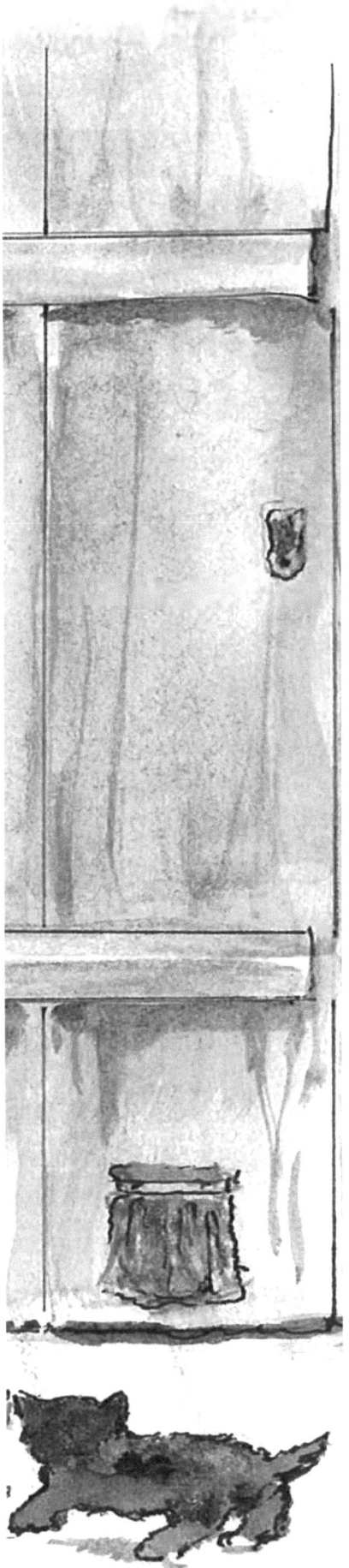

Spithead wondered what Isaac did at the top of those attic stairs.

Spithead cleaned house.

"What goes up must come down," Isaac said then he thought some more about gravity.

Why did things fall down instead of up or sideways, Isaac Newton wondered? "No great discovery was ever made without a bold guess."

Isaac thought about gravity for a long time. He said, "To arrive at the simplest truths requires years of comtemplation."

    Spithead and Isaac's time together was only for eighteen months, the duration of the Bubonic Plaque which was caused by a bacterium transmitted to a human by the bite of a flea.

Isaac Newton
1642-1727

about the author

CHARLOTTE MCKEE graduated from Crosbyton High School in 1963. She majored in English at West Texas A&M University located in Canyon, Texas. She taught high school English for one year and four year old children for seven years. A lifetime student of storytelling, Charlotte is a member of the Society of Children's Book Writers and Illustrtors (SCBWI). She spent her life in and around Arlington, Texas. This is her second published book.

about the illustrator

LINDA SHAW has enjoyed a lifetime career as an artist in various media. Her work appears across the country. In recent years she has illustrated a number of children's book. She finds it challenging and rewarding to transform the writer's vision into images which delight and stimulate the young reader.

also by Charlotte McKee

UNOPENED PRESENTS available from amazon.com

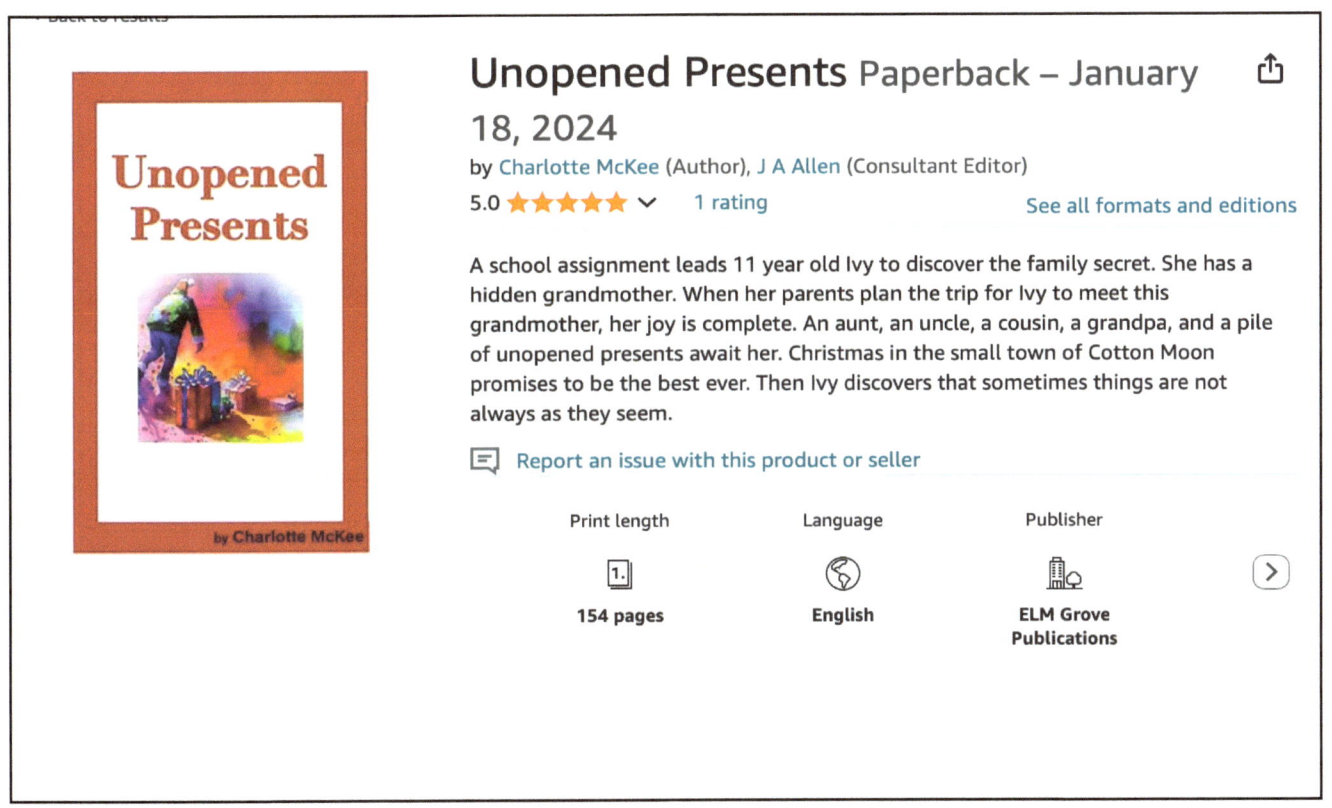

OR use the code to order directly

SPITHEAD! published by

ELM GROVE PUBLICATIONS

The Elm Grove Farm Series

Isabella the Cow Who Wanted to Sing
Henrietta the Hen Who Wouldn't Come In
Charlie the Pig Who Wanted to be Clean
Harvey the Horse Who Wanted a Hat
Snip the Lonesome Cowdog
Mama Yella and Her Kittysitters

J.B. Allen, author/publisher

Order SPITHEAD! through amazon.com,
or use the direct code.

ISBN 979-8-218-46848-4

www.ingramcontent.com/pod-product-compliance
Lightning Source LLC
Chambersburg PA
CBHW041411010526
44107CB00015B/1133